budgetbooks

CONTEMPORARY HITS

W9-DGA-814

ISBN 0-634-06732-X

HAL•LEONARD®
CORPORATION

7777 W. BLUEMOUND RD. P.O. BOX 13819 MILWAUKEE, WI 53213

Visit Hal Leonard Online at
www.halleonard.com

CONTENTS

AGAIN

Words and Music by
LENNY KRAVITZ

ALL MY LIFE

Words and Music by
FOO FIGHTERS

11

12

on to the next __ one. Done, __ done and I'm on to the next __ one. Done, __

__ done and I'm on to the next __ one. Done, __ done and I'm

on to the next __ one. Done, __ done and I'm on to the next __ one. Done, __

__ done and I'm on to the next __ one. Done, __ I'm done and I'm

ALL I HAVE

Words and Music by MAKEBA RIDDICK,
RONALD BOWSER, CURTIS RICHARDSON,
JAMES TODD SMITH, JENNIFER LOPEZ,
DAVE McPHERSON, LISA PETERS
and WILLIAM JEFFERY

Rap 2: *(See additional lyrics)*

Ain't noth-ing you can say__ to me that can change__ my mind. I've got-ta let you go now.

And noth-ing will ev-er be the same so just be on your way. Go 'head and do your__ thing now.

Additional Lyrics

Rap 1: It makes a cat nervous, the thought of settling down.
Especially me, I was creepin' all over town.
Thought my tender touch could lock you down.
I knew I had you as cocky as it sounds.
The way you used to giggle right before I put it down.
It's better when you're angry.
Come here I'll prove it now. Come here.

Rap 2: People make mistakes to make up, to break up, to wake up cold and lonely.
Chill baby, you know me.
You love me, I'm like your homey.
Instead of beefin', come hold me.
I promise I'm not a phony.
Don't bounce baby. Console me. Come here.

ALWAYS

Lyrics by JOSEY SCOTT
Music by BOB MARLETTE and JOSEY SCOTT

Original key: E♭ minor. This edition has been transposed up one half-step to be more playable.

AMAZED

Words and Music by MARV GREEN,
CHRIS LINDSEY and AIMEE MAYO

Moderately slow Country Ballad

Ev - 'ry time our eyes meet, this feel - in' in - side me
The smell of your skin, the taste of your kiss,

is al - most more — than I — can take. —
the way you whis - per in — the dark. —

*Recorded a half step lower.

32

I don't know how you do what you do.___ I'm so in love___ with you.._

It just keeps get-tin' bet ___ - ter.

I wan-na spend the rest of my life___ with you by my side___ for-ev-er and ev-

er.

Ev - 'ry lit - tle thing that you do,___

BEAUTIFUL

Words and Music by
LINDA PERRY

ANGEL

Words and Music by
SARAH McLACHLAN

Original key: Db major. This edition has been transposed down one half-step to be more playable.

BREATHE

Words and Music by HOLLY LAMAR
and STEPHANIE BENTLEY

CAN'T STOP LOVING YOU
(Though I Try)

Words and Music by
BILLY NICHOLLS

COME WHAT MAY

from the Motion Picture MOULIN ROUGE

Words and Music by
DAVID BAERWALD

Male: Nev-er knew I could feel___ like this,___ like I've___ nev-er seen___ the sky___

CLOCKS

Words and Music by GUY BERRYMAN, JON BUCKLAND,
WILL CHAMPION and CHRIS MARTIN

And noth - ing else com - pares.

D.S. al Coda
(with repeats)

COMPLICATED

Words and Music by AVRIL LAVIGNE, LAUREN CHRISTY,
SCOTT SPOCK and GRAHAM EDWARDS

CRY

Words and Music by
ANGIE APARO

DON'T KNOW WHY

Words and Music by
JESSE HARRIS

DRIVE

Words and Music by BRANDON BOYD,
MICHAEL EINZIGER, ALEX KATUNICH,
JOSE PASILLAS II and CHRIS KILMORE

Late - ly I'm _____ be - gin - ning to find __ that when __

D.S. al Coda

__ I drive __ my - self _____ my light ___ is found.

CODA

FALLIN'

Words and Music by
ALICIA KEYS

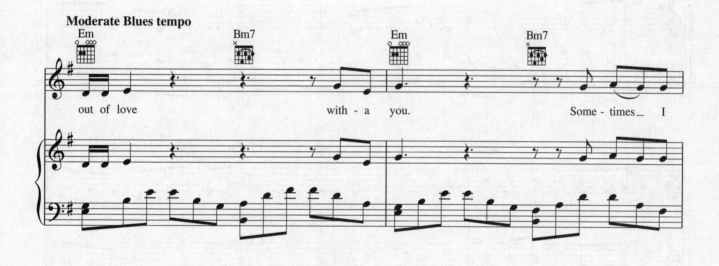

love with-a you. I _____ nev - er loved some - one _____ the way that

I love - a you. What?

DROPS OF JUPITER
(Tell Me)

Words and Music by PAT MONAHAN,
JIMMY STAFFORD, ROB HOTCHKISS,
CHARLIE COLIN and SCOTT UNDERWOOD

105

FLYING WITHOUT WINGS

Words and Music by WAYNE HECTOR
and STEVE McCUTCHEON

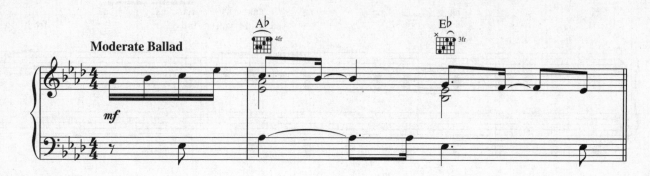

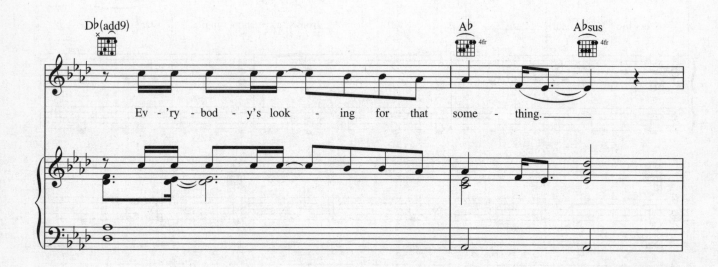

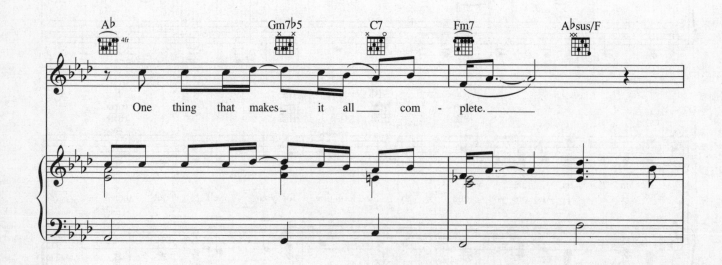

You'll find it in___ the strang - est plac - es.___

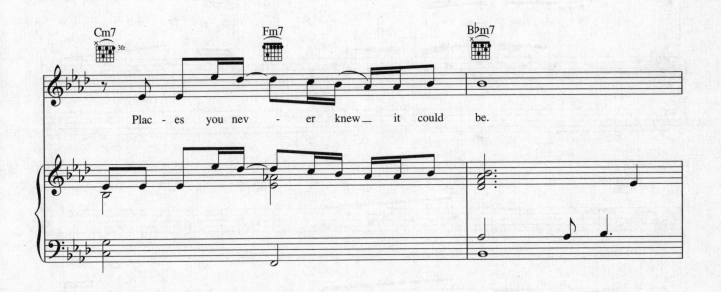

Plac - es you nev - er knew___ it could be.

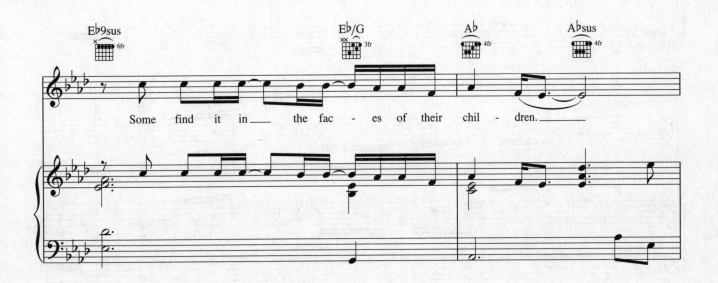

Some find it in___ the fac - es of their chil - dren.___

The kind you cher - ish all___ your___ life.

And when you know___ how much___ that means___ you've found that spe - cial

thing.___ You're fly - ing with - out wings.

So im - pos - si - ble as___ they may

seem, you've got to fight for ev - 'ry

dream. 'Cause who's to know which one you let

go would have made you com -

plete? But for me it's wak - ing up be - side you, yeah,

to watch the sun - rise on ___ your ___ face. ___

To know that I ___ can say I ___ love ___ you ___

at an - y giv - en time or ___ place, ___ oh. ___

FOLLOW ME

Words and Music by MATTHEW SHAFER
and MICHAEL BRADFORD

You don't know how you met me. You don't __ know __ why __ you __ can't __ turn a-round __ and say __ good-bye. __ All you know __ is when I'm with you I make you free __ and swim through your veins __ like a fish in the sea. __ I'm sing-in'

find no - bod - y else ___ like me. ___

Won't give you mon - ey, I can't give you the sky. ___

fol - low me _____ ev - 'ry - thing is all _____ right.

I'll be the one to tuck you in at _____ night. ___ And if you

want to leave _____ I can guar - an - tee ___ you won't ___

find no - bod - y else ___ like me. ___

THE GAME OF LOVE

Words and Music by RICK NOWELS
and GREGG ALEXANDER

Tell me ___

just what you want me ___ to be. ___
what-ev-er you make it ___ to be. ___

131

(Guitar Solo ad lib.)

(Make me feel good, yeah.)

HANGING BY A MOMENT

Words and Music by
JASON WADE

Medium Rock

Des - p'rate __ for chang - ing.
get - ting all __ I'm lack - ing. Com -

Starv - ing __ for truth. __ I'm
plete - ly in - com - plete. __ I'll

clos - er to where I start - ed.
take your in - vi - ta - tion.

* Recorded a half step lower.

Chas - ing   af - ter   you. _____ }
You take   all _____ of   me. _____ }

I'm fall - ing e - ven

* 2nd and 3rd times sing 8va (next 8 bars only)

Bm7   A   D   Bm7   A   D

more   in   love __ with   you. ___   Let - ting   go   of   all   I've   held __ on - to. ___

Bm7   A   D

___   I'm   stand - ing   here   un - til   you   make __ me   move. __   I'm   hang - ing   by   a

Bm7   A   D   1.

mo - ment   here __ with   you. ___

THE HARDEST THING

Words and Music by STEVE KIPNER
and DAVID FRANK

HERE'S TO THE NIGHT

Written by MAX COLLINS,
JON SIEBELS and TONY FAGENSON

148

HERO

Words and Music by ENRIQUE IGLESIAS,
PAUL BARRY and MARK TAYLOR

Spoken: *Let me be your hero.*

Would you

dance if I asked you to dance? _ Would you

I DRIVE MYSELF CRAZY

Words and Music by RICK NOWELS,
ELLEN SHIPLEY and ALLAN RICH

I DON'T WANT TO WAIT

Words and Music by
PAULA COLE

Repeat and Fade

Reprise theme of "Me"

I HOPE YOU DANCE

Words and Music by TIA SILLERS
and MARK D. SANDERS

hope you nev - er lose _____ your sense of won - der.
nev - er fear ___ those ___ moun - tains in the dis - tance.

I STILL BELIEVE

Words and Music by BEPPE CANTARELLI
and ANTONINA ARMATO

I WANT TO BE IN LOVE

Words and Music by
MELISSA ETHERIDGE

I'M WITH YOU

Words and Music by AVRIL LAVIGNE, LAUREN CHRISTY,
SCOTT SPOCK and GRAHAM EDWARDS

IF YOU HAD MY LOVE

Words and Music by RODNEY JERKINS,
LASHAWN DANIELS, CORY ROONEY,
FRED JERKINS and JENNIFER LOPEZ

IF YOU'RE GONE

Written by ROB THOMAS

IF YOU'RE GONE

I think you're wrong. __ I think you're al-read-y leav-ing. Feels like your hand is on __ the door. __ I thought this place was an em-pire. Now I'm re-laxed. __ I can't be sure. __ And I think you're so mean. __ I think we should try. __

IF I'M NOT MADE FOR YOU
(If You're Not the One)

Words and Music by
DANIEL BEDINGFIELD

IN A LITTLE WHILE

Words and Music by MATTHEW SHAFER
and MICHAEL BRADFORD

Here's to the good life or
On the oth-er side of a

so they say.___ All those par - ties and games___ that all those peo-ple play.___
coin there's a face. There's a mem-o-ry some - where___ that I can't e - rase.

They tell me this is the place___ to___ be.___ All these beau - ti - ful peo - ple and
And there's a place that I'll find___ some - day___ but some-times I___ feel___ like it's

D.S. al Coda

fin-'ly___ see.___ I just won - der, won - der if you think a-bout me.___

CODA

Yeah,_____ in a lit - tle while I'll be think - in' a-bout__ you.__

In a lit - tle while I'll still be___ here with-out__ you.__ You nev - er gave me a rea-

- son to doubt__ you.__ In a lit - tle while I'll be think - in' a-bout__ you ba-

INTUITION

Words and Music by JEWEL KILCHER
and LESTER A. MENDES

LANDSLIDE

Words and Music by
STEVIE NICKS

A MOMENT LIKE THIS

Words and Music by JOHN REID
and JORGEN KJELL ELOFSSON

Original key: C♯ minor. This edition has been transposed up one half-step to be more playable.

ONLY HOPE

from the Warner Bros. Motion Picture A WALK TO REMEMBER

Words and Music by
JONATHAN FOREMAN

Original key: C# minor. This edition has been transposed down one half-step to be more playable.

ONLY TIME

Words and Music by ENYA,
NICKY RYAN and ROMA RYAN

PEACEFUL WORLD

Words and Music by
JOHN MELLENCAMP

SMOOTH

Words by ROB THOMAS
Music by ROB THOMAS and ITAAL SHUR

SHE BANGS

Words and Music by DESMOND CHILD,
WALTER AFANASIEFF and ROBI ROSA

Instrumental solo

And if La - dy Luck _ gets on my side _ we're gon - na

SOAK UP THE SUN

Words and Music by JEFF TROTT
and SHERYL CROW

SUPERMAN
(It's Not Easy)

Words and Music by
JOHN ONDRASIK

THANK YOU

Words and Music by PAUL HERMAN
and DIDO ARMSTRONG

*Vocal written one octave higher than sung.

Original key: G# minor. This edition has been transposed up one half-step to be more playable.

Push the door; _ I'm home _ at _ last, _ and I'm soak - ing through _ and through. _

THIS IS THE NIGHT

Words and Music by GARY BURR,
ALDO NOVA and CHRISTOPHER BRAIDE

When the world was-n't up-side down,___ I could take all the time___ I had.___ But I'm not gon-na wait___ when a mo-ment can van-ish so fast. 'Cause

UNDERNEATH YOUR CLOTHES

Words and Music by SHAKIRA
Music co-written by LESTER A. MENDEZ

316

THIS KISS

Words and Music by ANNIE ROBOFF,
BETH NIELSEN CHAPMAN and ROBIN LERNER

UNDERNEATH IT ALL

Words and Music by DAVID A. STEWART
and GWEN STEFANI

THE WAY YOU LOVE ME

Words and Music by MICHAEL DULANEY
and KEITH FOLLESE

If

WHEREVER YOU WILL GO

Words and Music by AARON KAMIN
and ALEX BAND

(YOU DRIVE ME) CRAZY

Words and Music by JORGEN ELOFSSON,
MARTIN SANDBERG, PER MAGNUSSON
and DAVID KREUGER

WASTING MY TIME

Words and Music by DANNY CRAIG,
DALLAS SMITH, JEREMY HORA
and DAVE BENEDICT

wast - ing___ my___ time_____ a - gain,_____

oh,_____ a - gain._____